More Praise for
Cruisin' Passion Boulevard

These poems are classic Jonelle Maison, persona or personal, they provide great company on this rare snow day. They are more interesting than most poems on the range, they melt into me, from memory, by heart. Maison's sensibility ranges from cotillion to cottonwood, crotch rocket to Inuit tale, jaguars and sineaters, the intelligent music they make is a meld of deep south and high new Mexican. I suspect you will enjoy their width and depth as I do.

   —Joan Logghe
   Santa Fe Poet Laureate 2010-12

If you've ever ridden in a space shuttle, or the simulation of one, that's the ride Jonelle Maison's debut book takes us on—not the comfortable overview of the beautiful blue planet from outer space, but hurtling plunges into direct experience of earth's diverse natural world, culture and spirituality. Jonelle Maison is a Technician of the Mundane, Profane, and Sacred throughout time and these cultures, and she lands with us in a surprising conclusion—all of this in a slim volume of poetry! The vision and writing are breathtaking.

   —Jane Lipman
   Poet, *On the Back Porch of the Moon,*
   Winner of the 2013 New Mexico/Arizona Book Award and a NM Press Women's Award

Who among us legislators knew that the bill drafter we all liked the best, the drafter with the best prose, best grammar, best ability to write bills that were easy to understand, the one and only Jonelle Maison, was also a poet? Hiding in her office, working way past normal working hours to create laws we were proud of, but also, writing poetry? Poetry that assails the senses with alliterative sounds, figures of speech and evocative memories of the good ol' 60's when freedom was not just another word, but an American lifestyle to be embraced and celebrated. Jonelle's poetry takes us back down that road of freedom and fun and exhilaration, back to a time when we didn't work so much and thought about our lives in the present. It is so fun to go there with Jonelle.

—Mimi Stewart
NM Senator

Cruisin'
Passion Boulevard

Cruisin'
Passion Boulevard

Jonelle Maison

Cruisin' Passion Boulevard
Copyright ©2018 Jonelle Maison

ISBN: 978-0-578-41399-0
Publisher: Mercury HeartLink
Silver City, New Mexico
Printed in the United States of America

All rights reserved. This book, or sections of this book, may not be reproduced or transmitted in any form without permission from the author.

Permission is granted to educators to create copies of individual poems for classroom or workshop assignments with proper acknowledgment and credits.

Contact: jmaison@cybermesa.com

Cruisin' Passion Boulevard

II	More Praise for
	Cruisin' Passion Boulevard
XV	Acknowledgments
XVII	Invitation ~ Invocation: A Foreword
XXV	Gratitudes
1	Come to Me
2	Southern Baptist Sex, The '60s
4	Crotch Rockets
5	Cars in Love
6	National Poetry Week, 1990
8	Paper and Pens
9	Walking from Rubonia
10	Butter Could Never Go Rancid in This House
12	Years to Time, Going Home
14	What's Missing
16	The Story That Didn't Happen
17	A Childhood Recitation
18	When Otherwise I Forget,
	I Remember Love in Old Hotels
19	Form
20	Dream Rooms
22	Somewhere in My Twenties, Somewhere in My Thirties
23	An Answer from the Personals
24	"I Admire a Dust-Free Object"

25	FROM CHACO, MORE THAN MILES
26	SANI PASS
27	GOING TO THE BATHROOM IN THE CAPITOL
28	DAYDREAMING IN LIGHT AND MEMORY
30	IF I COULD BE OUTSIDE
32	SOME KNOWLEDGE SMARTER IN DOGS
37	THE DISHES CAN WAIT
38	IMAGINE A MARRIAGE
40	THANK YOU, BETH, FOR THE LASAGNA
41	TWO LADIES SHOPPING
41	THE SENTIENT DRESS
41	THE MILKY WAY IS MOVING AT 70 MILES PER SECOND
42	LEARNING THE WESTERN WAY
44	THERE ARE SAINTS IN THIS HOUSE
46	MARIE LAVEAU
48	HOODOO DEATH
50	THE SINEATER
54	THE BLUE FOLKS OF KENTUCKY
56	D N A
58	NOBODY BUT THE DEVIL: A MODERN FOLK TALE
64	THE WEAPONS OF WOMEN HAVE MANY USES
66	VISITING DAY AT THE PRISON FARM
67	FARM WIFE
68	A HELL OF A WOMAN
71	THERE'S SOME EVE IN EVERY WOMAN WHEN SHE EATS AN APPLE DURING BORING SEX
72	HOW DO HOLY WOMEN PICK THEIR CLOTHES?
74	THE QUEEN OF HEAVEN DEPOSED

76	Borrowed Knowledge
78	New Shoes
78	Danger!
79	Basket Weaver
80	Ritual for the Grandmother Stick
85	Moon in the Morning
86	The Girl Who Married a Dog
88	The Jaguar Man
92	The Jaguar Man's Wife, Ten Years Later
95	The Migration of Saints
98	Small Graces
100	The Maine Idyll Motor Court
103	About the Author

Acknowledgments

Ritual for the Grandmother Stick appeared in *The Woman Spirit Source Book* by Patrice Wynne, Harper & Row, Publishers, 1988.

Southern Baptist Sex, the '60s, Crotch Rockets, Farm Wife and *The Sineater* appeared in issues of the *Santa Fe Broadsheet*, edited by Linda Sperling.

A Hell of a Woman has traveled around the internet for years in Goddess circles.

The following poems were written specifically for readings: *National Poetry Week, Marie Laveau, Hoodoo Death, An Answer from the Personals, A Hell of a Woman, There's Some Eve in Every Woman When She Eats an Apple During Boring Sex, The Queen of Heaven Deposed* and *The Jaguar Man*.

Invitation ~ Invocation: A Foreword

You have in hand a multifaceted gem of a book, a peach, pure pleasure spilling onto page. These vivid poems are lyrical, oratory; this is poetry that is meant to be heard: meant to be said aloud, so the effortless musicality will sing straight into your ears.

These are poems that I have myself heard, many many times, in Jonelle Maison's nuanced and electrifying performances; poems, that like the poet herself, I dearly love.

Poems in a thoroughly honed Voice, capable of range and the swift downshift: feisty, fearless, then silken; bawdy and boisterous…then achingly tender.

This is poetry that takes us back to an eager, bad-girl '60s, back and through passion,

> *In that buttercup yellow Rambler*
> *I thought we'd be together forever.*
> *A three on the column*
> *and ready for love.*

and lack of it,

> *I've milked this damn cow*
> *now for years before breakfast.*
> *Skin like old shoes, my hands do not stick*
> *to winter metal. I move the biscuits*
> *without flinching.*

to the South, making heat and humidity,

> ...*like oranges, like blossoms,*
> *like the air in the groves on a hot summer night.*

rise steaming from the page.

This is poetry rooted deeply in time, showing us Maison's past with the unflinching clarity born of deep allegiance, alliance.

> *I pass the gladiola farms,*
> *acres of death wreaths smirking in the summer sun.*
> *See Ba-pa's uniform empty, laid out in white satin*
> *just gloves & shoes & head surrounded by pink condolences.*

Never a poet to shy from telling the hard stories, the work lifts us past mere personal revelation through deep craft, seamlessly seeking and achieving Eliot's "objective correlative" through utterly apt metaphor.

> *The sideboard is splitting apart.*
> *Dishes break like the marriage of potters.*
> *The yard is full of rocks.*
>
> *Everywhere there is danger.*
> *I cannot cook. Soon, I will have to lock the car*
> *and walk.*
>
> *Here, everything is sprung out of shape.*
> *I wear confusion like an old house dress*
> *bought for its faded bouquets of violets*
> *and lily of the valley, your favorites.*

These are poems rooted in place, bringing us also, in exact and loving detail, to the poet's beloved New Mexico.

Look
at the grasses, big bluestem,
grama, galleta, see them praying
with each exhalation of world breath.

And poetry that knows intimately the huge Unknown yawning beyond our fingers reaching for the light switch.

I drive with shadows
that cannot touch, cannot hurt,
toward a dimension further away
than putting on my nightgown, turning off the lights.

These are poems that sweep us out and away…and in…into the archetypal, the mythic: her métier, the Mystery. Poems still rich with physicality, lush with image, with story, and poured through the fervent scholarship of a Lover.

Maison takes on the Holy, and here you will find portraits, in sassy vernacular, of the Divine Feminine: Goddesses and Saints,

It's the women, the Marys and Marthas, who cook the dinners
where only one out of ten popes says thank you or your best.

and

Dymphna is too crazy to eat.
She ran from her father who was so pagan he could even see
past the fog of the angels.

of Eve

> *Oh, not eating the apple. It was too delicious.*
> *Or flirting with that snake. One bite & she knew he knew*
> *some pretty thrilling tricks.*
> *The tongue alone, she dreamed about for years.*

and Lilith.

> *Tell God for me*
> *this fight goes on as long as it must.*

Folk tales of hoodoo and voodoo, but poignant and insistently real, tales of the Sineater,

> *My name is Levee Buckingham.*
> *Sometimes I forget.*
> *When the last of the old folks go*
> *there won't be no one to remind me.*

of Marie Laveau,

> *My eyes are half moons,*
> *won't die till they're full.*
> *They are the eyes of my mother's mother*
> *below her seven-knotted tignon*

and the power wrought by true magic

> *When I Fix you, don't matter what you think*
> *I be slippin' underneath, to the jungle*
> *behind your eyes.*

by the *high yeller woman* that took on poor Cotton Williams.

> *Got herself a bit of Fast Luck Water*
> *an a Black Cat Bone. She be wearin some Follow Me Oil,*
> *make the Four Corners in the graveyard at night*
> *but ain't nothin git my Cotton come away from his ways.*

Maison has the knack of quiet celebration, of seeing the milagro in the Ordinary, and stretching her lines into sentences that hold her deft metrics, making a different music in prose poems, as in this poem in praise of writing.

> *Moving very, very slowly back and forth till I had covered the white sheets completely with the black ink. I kissed the page over and over.*

Certainly, the constant in this collection, is the poet's scope, offering us also poems reminding us of the simple, the daily, way to hold inside long-time loving.

> *We hike into town, buy dinner in cans,*
> *come back holding hands.*
> *Afterwards, we move the rocking chairs closer together,*
> *listen to the night before we go in, turn off the light.*

And always, the subtext of all Maison's work, is a deep honoring of the Sacred, and recognition of the necessity of personal, individually enacted Ritual, the way of Women, of Poets, of Celebrators throughout time and culture.

Take these words literally:

> *As you circle*
> *in the earth circle*
> *match your heart*

to the drum
let your bracelets sound
these words
let them enter you as fire,
as water.

This poet means what she says.

—Judyth Hill
  Autumn 2018

Gratitudes

I met Judyth Hill and Joan Logghe in a poetry workshop a long time ago and their friendship changed the trajectory of my life. Jane Lipman, who had the Taos Institute and brought brilliant people like Gioia Timpanelli, Robert Bly and Joseph Campbell for weekend workshops was also part of that transformative time. I thank them from the bottom of my heart.

This book is the result of Judyth pushing and pulling and pushing some more. I am beyond grateful. There is nothing I could do to ever repay her deep generosity to me.

All gratitude and love go to my husband, Laird Graeser, who has loved and supported me through everything—even my very many years as the Menopausal Bitch of the Western World. It's a miracle I'm still married —thanks, my dearest Laird.

Come to Me

Come to me in yellow,
like a beacon in a hurricane
before the eye has passed over
or like oranges, like blossoms,
like the air in the groves on a hot summer night.

Come to me like a sad country tune
played in a near-empty bar in Tucumcari, NM,
like the bruised mauve sky over Route 66 and
Gallup on an early winter evening
before Christmas and we're heading west
to light, to ocean, to oranges.

Or come to me like the deep green inside
of an F150 pickup, the fanciest package:
cloth seats, air conditioning & music.
Come to me like jeans & a T-shirt
faded & ready for stroking
the zipper bent in that way of men
that stops my heart
makes me want to travel,
wish I was a waitress again.

Southern Baptist Sex, The '60s

We wuz cruisin'
Passion Boulevard
& I just knew he was the One.
My Fabian.
My Dreamboat.

That boy, so cute
in his pelvis riders & DA
hadda 3-D crotch ya couldn't miss
pointin' always to the future.
Makes me shiver.

Uh huh!
He turn them bedroom eyes on me
& goose bumps all over start risin',
Baptist Training Union pledges gone
right on outta my head.

Oh Lordy,
I try to 'member last Sunday's sermon
or Sister
& her Unfortunate Mistake
but ooh whee sugar
how I 'member such
when I be creamin' in my panties
as he kiss me them deep
Soulful kisses,
stick his tongue in my ear?

I cudda died for him.
Wuz takin' Home Ec for him.

I just knew it wuz love:
he gimme his Future Farmers jacket.
I let him undo my bra

Crotch Rockets

Good Girls didn't ride motorcycles.
Stuck to horses if they were lucky
or played that game their girlfriend learned
when she visited her cousins in Ohio —
you know the one.

Good girls didn't straddle 74s
with fringed saddlebags,
didn't feel the white cotton T-shirt
close as hope, soft as a sigh, or
the sharp corners of a Marlboro box rolled in the sleeve.
Good girls didn't know Fruit of the Loom
could be so good.

Good girls didn't dream
of hugging a boy that way,
pelvis tucked into the curve of an older,
smarter behind:
one that knows more than is safe
for a girl who goes to cotillion,
keeps a hope chest.

But honey,
reputation can't be everything
or we'd be a generation of women
who still can't name the parts of the body
that love motorcycles.

All over America
even in Ohio
women are moaning to their husbands:

Thrill me like a Harley.

Cars in Love

In that buttercup yellow Rambler
I thought we'd be together forever.
A three on the column
and ready for love.

I knew we could grow old together,
driving down country roads
while I gave you head —
a game to see what comes first:
you or the fence at the turnoff.

Was it to be the orange groves
or home,
your turn in the lake?
Thank God,
you could hold your breath a long time.

Then it was over.
You took my Rambler to her house
gave me a push-button Dodge,
slant 6, my future.

Now there was a car that wanted to go cross country,
yearned for a drier climate,
taller men,
and lesbians.

National Poetry Week, 1990

I discovered e.e. cummings in 1961
and found poetry.

It was eleventh grade, I worked in the school library.
I was in love with Dr. Tom Dooley, wanted to go to Vietnam
sew the ears back on south Vietnamese villagers
or run a Southern Baptist orphanage.

But then I read e.e. cummings
and found poetry.

It was like Saul, hit in the head with lightning
on the road to Damascus and lying in the dirt.

I quit the library and hung out in study hall
with the rackey boys, learned to dance.
I smoked marijuana on old 301
with Karl who balanced on his father's head upside down
in the circus, and there was no going back.

This was nothing like English class,
Mrs. Skinner reading the Cavalier Poets in quavering voice,
the farm boys sleeping, the beauty queens passing notes
and trying on lipsticks.

Uh huh, here was something I couldn't believe:
poetry that walked and talked — that strutted
past the First Baptist Church in everybody's town.
Here was something that said out loud
what white girls felt the first time we saw Elvis.

Soon, there would be the beats:
Ferlinghetti, Corso, Di Prima,
A Sailor at Midnight and Anne Sexton,
William Carlos, T.S. and Frost, Lorca and Ernesto Epistola,
a cellist and conductor who still lives in Sarasota,
not that I knew that.
There would be so many more,
and even, now, a feeling for the Cavalier Boys.

But that first time. Reading cummings.
I was fat and had bad skin, but just then,
just for a moment,
I knew about
right now.

PAPER AND PENS

I remember when ballpoint pens first came out, and I stole one. I got caught, of course. My mother made me take it back and say I was sorry, but I wasn't. How could I be sorry holding that silver smooth cylinder, slightly cool and warming to my touch. It had a clip, but I didn't understand it. If I had I could have only clipped it on my pajama shirt in the dark late at night or on my shorts in the closet where I played dolls, not in public. The button made a satisfying popping sound, like gum, years later when I learned to snap it as I chewed. But back to that button. Click and the point came down ready to do my bidding. Click, it retreated, waiting in metallic patience for me to come back.

I'm not even sure I was old enough to write, I think not. But still, I knew that here was something important in my life. Here was a way to love myself. I remember standing in front of that jewelry store case, I remember, even today sitting in the age of Uniball Indelibles in four shades of mauve, orange and green, I remember how much my heart wanted those pens. My fingers felt the siren call. I needed one of those pens. I reached out, slowly, not even knowing what would happen, I reached out and touched it, picked it up. It was just as I imagined. In the closet I held it and clicked it on, off, on, off. Stroked pieces and pieces of paper with it. Back and forth. Moving very, very slowly back and forth till I had covered the white sheets completely with the black ink. I kissed the pages over and over.

WALKING FROM RUBONIA
for my sister, Carol

I remember that walk from Rubonia
past midnight, we just kept walking.
Miles added on one, two, eight, eleven
we walked, our white tennis shoes like lanterns
we followed. We were young and tanned
found our way by moonlight and Villager.

Isn't it funny, the moments we were close:
a day in Andersonville, one day
that time you lived alone, and
walking from Rubonia.

Butter Could Never Go Rancid in This House

Silence congeals the roast beef,
frosts the sensitive leaves of brussels sprouts.

Butter could never go rancid in this house.

They sit on either side of the doorway,
eat slowly for the time it will take up.
Tired eyes stir the salad,
desires roll around the plate with the peas.
Resignation is a gravy to sop.

After dinner she works crossword puzzles,
he watches TV.

What is an eight-letter word for what we are?

Twenty-seven years
have simplified the mathematics of their lives,
sandpapered the pronouns down
to first person singular.
They divvied up the house between them
like the last slice of pie.

And the hours. Hers, the day
his, the night. The passion of the early years
replaced
by beds thin as hope.

The nightstand's neutrality
casts a shadow where slippers never sleep.

Nine thousand eight hundred and fifty-five days.

The time of melting through is imprecise
but sure. 1 divided by 2 is nothing

but its own damn answer.
Do they mourn the death of pronouns?

Years to Time, Going Home

Near the Ruskin tomato fields
is a curve I never want to turn
so easy to continue, soft
with my mother settling into my body,
a dream neither of us has had.

I pass the gladiola farms,
acres of death wreaths smirking in the summer sun.
See Ba-pa's uniform empty, laid out in white satin
just gloves & shoes & head surrounded by pink condolences.

From the years' reverie
I drive stretches of highway
between Tampa & home.
Going through Gibsonton
palm trees & circus freaks
vie for the skyline.
Walgreens is full of them.

I sip a coke beside the Lobster Boy
eating his kin on the daily special,
think of the orchids grown by Raiford prisoners.

The Armless Man
& his friend with no legs
ride their bicycle, race me to the city limits.
The scenery turns flat once more
color dulls out with miles of scrub palms
& a man in the next lane waving his tongue at me
like a "Welcome Y'all!" sign in a hick town.

More miles in a hum state, images without glue,
I gun it down the dip to the interchange, flash past Palmetto
& I'm on the Manatee Bridge, almost home.
Streets of childhood in yellow half-light make me ache,
I try for ways to rephrase history
looking for a yes or no answer.

By the time I pull in the driveway
I am refracted into mirage,
feel like the palm trees
dying from imported diseases.

What's Missing

Here, there are no azaleas clustering under the eaves
or dogwoods showing the stigmata on each petal.
No camellias sway in the river breeze,
a scent spilling over towards hope.

Here, there is a mother dead almost a year.

Here, there is silence that won't end,
the silence of years that will not be explained now.
Love that cannot be understood on the tongue.

It is the silence after the last harsh intake
of air — an air empty of nourishment,
empty of our voices
crying for you to love us.

We are a family that does not last beyond the last breath.

I am lost in the silence.
Made stupid by secrets.

The sideboard is splitting apart.
Dishes break like the marriage of potters.
The yard is full of rocks.

Everywhere there is danger.
I cannot cook. Soon, I will have to lock the car
and walk.

Here, everything is sprung out of shape.
I wear confusion like an old house dress
bought for its faded bouquets of violets
and lily of the valley, your favorites.

In my dreams, there is no fur.
Only reptiles, restless in their mass,
the cruel odor of crushed orange blossoms.

Here, time does not change. Pain resides in the palm,
streaks toward the heart like venom.
Indelible xxx's mark the journey.
Like the fairy tales, each night
I sprinkle cornmeal at all the doorsteps
in the morning, it lies twisted and scattered:
the footprints of love
between mother and daughter.

The Story That Didn't Happen

My mother is sweet and hates sex. She wears aprons, bakes cookies, won't allow us out of the house without a kiss. In this story, my mother has skin that feels like love, the color of inherited pearls, that strand she wears every day. She is softer than the foxtails on a gray jersey dress in this story, kinder than azaleas banked against oak trees and green lawns, welcome shade on a hot Georgia afternoon. My mother grows old gracefully, has friends and a family who cannot stay away. My mother laughs, has no regrets, and keeps up the grave of her father. She has always loved us. She writes me letters each week, tells of gardening, how the jasmine smells at dusk walking along the river with a full heart, a desire to see. There is no confusion between a mother and daughter in this story. Here, we know where we are. Here, I rest my head on her breast while she strokes my hair. I can feel it in my own chest. Just below the collarbone it spreads with a spiral motion like a burrowing animal, blind and searching for home. When it reaches the palm, fingers curl down, hold on. Finally, it is the palm that remembers. Even here, in that other story, is the palm of wounds, the stigmata of family.

A CHILDHOOD RECITATION
For my sister, Sandy

When I was little
a snake
fell on my head.

Well...actually
it fell on my sister's
head.

Well...really
it wasn't
a snake.

It was a limb.

Well...maybe
it was only
a leaf.

Well...I guess
it wasn't anything
at all

   just the wind

rustling round the house
me
safely in bed.

When Otherwise I Forget, I Remember Love in Old Hotels

Lies and love live in the body
common as blood.
We make our way from memory
in the rooms of old hotels.

Common as blood,
the secrets of ghosts remain
in the rooms of old hotels.
We breathe them in with the dust.

The secrets of ghosts remain
coiling around us in the night.
We breathe them in with the dust,
A drought that will not end.

Coiling around us in the night
lies and love live in the body
a drought that will not end.
We make our way from memory.

FORM

I'm searching for form,
some shape to our history.
I hear the form of death
between breaths and I cannot escape.
Kin gives a shape that marriage never can
rhythm in the blood knows when to lift,
to throw.

I write prose now, stretching out the lines toward form.
What is free form to the lost?
Pantoums I try, but do not succeed.
It's the repeating lines I don't get,
the anxiety of views.

I yearn for form like a rookie yearns to slide for home
in the big game.
Or the dancer, *plie, plie, sur les pointes.*

In acrobatics, form is the teacher.
When you hold your legs together,
you spin slower & cannot see
where you are going.
That is a good thing to know.

I didn't kiss you on the lips,
could not call you mother.

My form now is grief.

Dream Rooms

We've had the same dream,
my friend and I.
The one where we're waitresses
again, in an old house
with leaded glass windows
and narrow oak floors.

Everything is antique,
even the lace tablecloths bought
from an estate, whose I'm sure I know.

The family
still lives upstairs.

The empty apartment grandmother left
to her son, the second dad.
He lies in bed, sick,
soon to die.

On his back porch my father
lives as a wolf.
He leaps at me when I come out
to check the weather.

The chain holds his leap,
thick links of tradition.
I feel his breath lunge
around hot teeth.

I say, *Back!* and he goes.
My heart blooms with triumph.

But this is a bigger house than it looks.

There are the rooms of the dangerous uncles.
Rapists in two generations, unacknowledged bond
between mother and daughter.

Then I turn.

At the end of the hall stands
my mother's apartment.
I cannot feel whether she is home.
It gleams, draws me,
welcome or fear,
who can interpret a dream?
I don't go there.

I say, I want to see the rooms
that could be mine.
Even now, I think of living there.

As I move through them
I feel the worry growing
like hard breathing,
thoughts drawn to the hall.

This dream will end soon,
I won't have time to find
where my mother lives.

Somewhere in My Twenties, Somewhere in My Thirties

Somewhere in my twenties
I was feeding my path to sea gulls
without a glance at their diving
from make-believe palm trees
as I laid myself down
on the mattresses of the Aquarian Age.

Somewhere in my thirties
you still want things to be simple,
want stars to be innocent of death.
You pretend that our history is carried
in a set of matched luggage, their fine leather
scraped clean of blood
and the hint of mortality.

While you were married
and unpacked all those years,
my baggage kept growing, heavy and graceless,
stuffed in croaker sacks,
beat-up cartons from the back of liquor stores
and a couple of trunks stickered with places I'll never see.

Now, somewhere near forty
there is not enough room for your stranger's hand to be
where it is.

An Answer from the Personals

LOOKING for SWF 35/50, good condition for hiking, rafting,
mountain biking. Romantic evenings in a hot tub.

Sorry. I'm not looking for that kind of exercise.
I've been outdoors.
I wanna feel the kitchen floor on my thighs,
impress the wall with my backside.

Your ad had too many things for us to do.
& too much water,
though I know we women are supposed to like that.
I only want to lie in bed with the fan on,
lick favorite liqueurs off each other's body.
By candlelight, of course, if you insist.
I know I said I wanted romance —
but it's not what you think.
I don't wanna hear those tired old lines,
or eat nouvelle in a pastel room,
us staring, soulfully, over glasses
of what I'm too embarrassed to ask,
"white Grenache?"

No, honey. Moans will do,
the abstract of love.
Johns & Rothko will have nothing on us.
We can be one step beyond
the last shell Georgia O'Keefe painted.

You know that ribbon of highway she painted,
clearer and clearer each time?
That's what I wanna feel. And those hills.
Let's not forget the possibility of those hills.

"I Admire a Dust-Free Object"

Joan says.
So rich a phrase,
perfect & evocative.

"I admire a dust-free object"
pushes Time off the linear continuum
& puts it where it belongs:
a shawl of possibilities fringed
long enough
for nervous fingers to play in.

Do you hear the Great Civilizations
in those words?
Do you hear our history?
Boldly,
this sentence tap dances
across the pros & cons,
ballets through our days
a little ragtime,
sometimes rock 'n' roll,
certainly the blues
& Beethoven's mathematical agreement.

Women live in this world
bounded by museums
& mental hospitals,
confused by the two.

From Chaco, More Than Miles

On the backside of the sunset
clouds bleed through from some other time.
The landscape is almost familiar,
places we used to know, or saw
driving by in greener moods,
but there is an alien twist here
to the light, the shape of mountain,
like the eyes of a feral woman
we cannot look into, or be caught.

Steel will not grip here.
Nothing stands higher than the hills
lying over someone's lost home.
It is the arrogance of automobiles
that thinks we move through a plain air,
traveling with ears deaf
to the hymns of the old heroes.

The language of the first moon
is the speech of this place.
It calls to our dreams
as the tides call our blood
over the memory of three times drowning.
We know this land in the fleeting moment
between breaths, nearly
our bodies hear the words spoken in sleep
of this far country we think to hold in a snapshot.

Sani Pass
for Koos Prinsloo

Coming to Lesotho by Sani Pass
I think of the terminator, that moon line
between dark and light. The edge of a country.

Topping out, we could be on the moon.
Aliens, we are dumb in this place.
Speech is the least language here,
where air and stone have their own vocabulary.
Wind pushes us like a harridan, giving orders:
Go there, now!

In the sharp beauty of afternoon, the footprints of old stories
are there in the dust, calling us to spirit
calling us to remember.

There is a feather on the moon.
It could have come from here.

Going to the Bathroom in the Capitol

Euphemia dates the toilet paper rolls.
Muttering witch words,
she marks them like the sun
with six rays
then hides them in the ashtray.

Processo steals them,
she tells me,
to sell in Truchas.
Don't worry though,
she says,
nothing for you to worry about.

But still,
I do. Worry.
Sometimes a shiver of fear
electrocutes my clitoris,
currents up my rectum
& I feel snakes crawling toward my throat.

When I vomit snails & toads
I just sigh.
Oh Euphemia, you crazy old bat,
you got the spell wrong
again.

Daydreaming in Light and Memory

On viewing *Bringing in the Boats* by A.G. Rider

In the desert, I sit watching fishermen
pull their boats from the surf.
There is salt in the air
reminding me of an afternoon
drinking tea with Eugenie Shonnard.
She talked about the light in Brittany.
Different from France, she said, it's from the sea.
But her art held more the memory of land,
aboriginal understanding of rabbit, deer and pueblo faces.

Her conversation then saw no difference
between last week and any summer
on the New England coast.
In the dining room
she stroked the dark grain of the table,
talked of the first time her mother let her drink
from the cup she now held in her hand.
"Brittany blue," she said, holding it delicately up
between the deceitful fingers of old age.
"This color, so full of my life."

We moved through her house on the Paseo like years,
back and forth,
as she told her story in furniture and china.
In my own house now, I see that. It is the house
of a woman whose mother has died.
The weight of history in sideboard and silver.

That day, I ached for my grandmothers. Their stories,
the lace and gestures that set them in the memory.
Like Eugenie, my mind wove in time and persons
the intricate pattern of family.

Studying Rider's fishermen, there is nothing obvious
like light or line that leaps over
to Eugenie's stone art and that shared day, just
this:
memories are the steel blue of weathering sea,
of shadow when light shines through the thinnest porcelain.

Eugenie Shonnard (1886-1978) was an internationally recognized painter and sculptor. She studied painting with Alphonse Mucha in New York and painting and sculpture with Emile-Antoine Bourdelle and Auguste Rodin in Paris. She moved to Santa Fe in 1927 and became very interested in Pueblo Indians. She developed a material, similar to sandstone, from which she sculpted Indian figures and animals; she also sculpted many garden fountains. She was commissioned by the federal government to do art projects for the WPA during the Depression.

If I Could Be Outside
During the Legislative Session

If I could be outside, I would not
wash the dishes or hang up my clothes,
I wouldn't dust or sweep or
sit at my desk

If I could be outside, I might lie
under the Mountain Spirit, look up his skirt,
drink coffee at Ohori's or hang with the ducks at Fenn's

I'd move farther and farther and farther away
if I could be outside, from the capitol
to an art gallery and beyond

If I could be outside I'd move toward wilderness,
toward the scent of dawn
and brutal fur, I'd move
to trees like a dancer, not tango
or waltz but older, past
any civilization of steps and pattern
to movement that starts in the heart
and pushes into the limbs as a thick tide of salty desire,
a dance of fewer and fewer clothes

If I could be outside I would look for water
and rocks and love, what I
used to know before architecture and symphonies

I would walk for miles just to feel
the rough path in my calves.
There could be nothing about thinking in this
or stories about clouds,
if I could be outside
breathing, the absence of walls and heavy books
deep in the mountains
I'd lie down and listen.

Some Knowledge Smarter in Dogs

     I
I take the dog out, look up.
The stars come upon me
unprepared. I feel pregnant
with the whole sky. Beyond all horizons.

Flamboyant, mysterious
they glow in the raven dark sky.
They are so close.
Inhaling, I am filled with starlight,
feel it moving through me like heat lightning
on a hot summer night.

I search for gods and heroes striding around,
look for the Seven Sisters,
Venus and Cassiopeia,
Taurus the Bull,
names without reference,
I look blindly, unknowing
but, still, I feel the grace surrounding me.

I stand rooted, cannot move   .
don't feel the tug of leash.
The half moon is so bright
the whole circle shines,
I'd never noticed there's a halo of stars around it.
Surely they have names, or one name. Holy Nimbus.
The Milky Way lives up to its name:
a white moustache of worlds
smeared across the sky.

I am surrounded by stars. I am in stars.
How is it that what we are a part of
seems so separate, so far away?

I know the names of the moon.
This is August, Green Corn moon, Grain moon,
half full in the southern sky.
Halfway between Albuquerque and Santa Fe
it shines on this landscape that has splurged
into green this rainy year.
Indian gourds linger on the vine
and grass heads wave in this sweet night's breeze.

I forget to breathe.

    II
Molly Tamale pulls on the leash.
Look around you! she orders,
it's not just about stars.
Look at those trees over there,
dusty and forest greens,
needles and fringes,
how they belong. Look
at the grasses, big bluestem,
grama, galleta, see them praying
with each exhalation of world breath.

Feel that breath on your own skin,
feel the world not divided between
natural and human.
See the footprints left in rocks and dust.

Where you are standing has been here
and occupied for ages uncounted,
don't think yours is the first house on this land.
There used to be water where sand and rocks
have lived now for a century or two,
and camping fires all over the meadow.
You are not so far away from ancient pueblos:
you've built in their backyard.

Before them, there were coyotes,
the ancestors of those who live here now,
who sing you to sleep
in the slowly darkening night.
There were the same redtail hawks and shining magpies,
flickers jumping around in the air.
Roadrunners stalked mice and house finches
in the door yard.

Don't forget the ravens, like you see every day
riding wind currents, tasting prayers and incense
on the air. Messengers. Bringers of light out of
darkness, crying *tomorrow, tomorrow*
to those who listen.

Always, there were rocks, they are nothing new.
Here are the ones that saw the Great Uplift
of the Sangre de Cristos
and the volcanic explosion of the Jemez.
This place is one gigantic rock, its taproot deep
past the crust, burrowing through the mantle

a ledge of rock that talks to itself.
You could hear if you laid down on it
like I do. Learn to praise it!

The world, when it was still only one, saw
everything living here.

    III
The Pueblo Indians believe that houses,
like everything else in this world,
are born from the earth, live and then die.
They welcome the honor to live in such a house.

I shall honor mine too, built by the hands
of my husband, a gift I haven't repaid.
I can't help it, this mixture of praise and practicality,
loving what is here, I still say, *when will the deck...*
or *we need...*say, *could we please
finish the bathroom?*

In precious praise moments, I feel them.
Past occupants of this lot surrounded by mountains.
I could reach out, touch them
walking past, hunting rabbits,
my coyotes, the occasional deer.

Squinting with starlight I see them
looking the same then
as they do now,
except without pick-up trucks
parked at the doors.

Maybe everything was richer before roads
and electrical boxes,
before houses built for permanence.
Who knows?

Live in your time without envy
Molly Tamale says,
or change your ways.

THE DISHES CAN WAIT

The dishes can wait.
It's Southern Comfort on the rocks at the Eldorado Bar
a rainy August evening,
the kind of day where you drag out
autumn clothes, start an anxiety:
daylight savings time is almost gone.

The dishes can wait.
In just a little while, this weather
will go from charming to serious.
In just a little while we'll be contemplating
murder-suicide pacts with strangers, begin
burning out the high numbers on the electric blanket,
in progressive, descending order.

If 7 burns out on Groundhog's Day,
does that mean 5 goes before Spring?

But now, the dishes can wait.
It's still summer. These clothes are hot
after all, too hot.
The dishes can wait. It's still daylight
and I have friends.

Imagine a Marriage
For Julia and Eddy, September 26, 2015

Weddings cry out for small appliances,
for china and silver, egg cups and fish knives
but I offer this poem instead of a toaster
or yet another hand mixer,
I offer a glimpse of possible marriage
instead of a place setting or a silver hostess set
with asparagus forks and celery servers.

Imagine a marriage.

Imagine a bedroom, Coral Blush
satin finish, a gift from husband to wife
her favorite color, soft as the deep inside of the
seashell her father brought home from war.
Imagine an iron bedstead covered
in white chenille, made up traditionally each day
over two flat bed pillows, two hand-crocheted pillows
one round, one square, on top.

Imagine the picture of a favorite saint,
Therese of the flowers, overhead
and only one night table in the small room.
You know the single curtain is lace,
a wedding present from her mother and aunt.

Imagine a marriage.

When you see that bed, the room,
 you know about marriage.
You know that the man and woman who share it
have loved one another for over fifty years.

They have raised a family of many children,
grandchildren and great-grands,
they sleep tucked next to each other every night,
still hold hands walking to church or sitting
on the portal in the sweet color of evening.

They gave everything worth giving to their family
by example, by love.
They speak fluently the secret dialect of couple,
of kiss and whisper, touch and shadow.

They always know where the other is,
not because they demand it, but because
they feel it.
If you saw their eyes when they look at each other
you would recognize your own commitment,
your own longing for the other.

What you imagine says everything
about love's clichés and complications.
It says what everyone says,
how loving is hard, and easy, too.
It says, when you see the Beloved
You are standing in the sacred.

May your own marriage look like this.

Thank You, Beth, For the Lasagna

It was so delicious
I could not stop myself.
I ate the whole amount, not intended
but kept on eating
eating, eating, smaller and smaller bites
I savored, I savored to the tongue's last flick of sauce
from the container, the fork lying naked, clean.
I thank you
this brief vacation in Italy,
it was a moment in Sicily or the mountain towns while I ate,
poured some wine,
sliced fruit and cheese for dessert,
spoke Italian in my dreams.

Two Ladies Shopping

You look so good in blue,
I always think of you
wearing green.

The Sentient Dress

Low-cut hibiscus clutches her body
in tight embrace more familiar than skin,
rides every curve and movement
like a satisfying lover.

The Milky Way is Moving at 70 Miles Per Second

Hey, slow down, pal,
it feels like a hurricane
down here!

Learning the Western Way

There are too many paths, too many maps.

Too much to know
in any lifetime.

I gotta specialize.

From now on,
I'm only traveling from Greece, west.

At every fork, I'll erect
universal direction signs:
a bar through the picture of
Rajneesh
the Buddha
Lao Tzu.

It was easy for Sleeping Beauty.
She had her epiphany in a kiss.
Me, I'm still yawning.

When there is no prince in sight
to bring back time,
when you don't wake up till you're thirty-five
you gotta specialize.

My body knows the Western path.
It is easy being blonde. I remember blue.
Something recognizes grandmother's footprints
in the dust.

Synapses fire to hear Athena, Artemis,
Hecate, leap at the mention of
Bronwyn and Morgan La Fey,
but say Vishnu, Krishna, Confucius
and I am blank,
my ears can't translate such exotic sounds.

Too many paths, too many maps,
There's not enough time.
I gotta specialize.

Moving ever Westerly,
I'll listen to those old songs
my blood knows by heart.
My blood knows
by heart.

There Are Saints in this House

There are saints in this house.
They walk beside you, jostle
to get to the next room.
Often, there are so many

you can't get out of their way.

There are saints in this house.
Some are too deep to watch you
or be seen. You'll almost
hear them pray or talk amongst themselves,
sometimes you'll feel the slight tremor of holy laughter.
It feels like a hand drawing a blessing on your heart.

It's the women, the Marys and Marthas, who cook the dinners
where only one out of ten popes says thank you or your best.
Says yummm.

Dymphna is too crazy to eat.
She ran from her father who was so pagan he could even see
past the fog of the angels. As she ran, country
to ocean to land, she prayed to be saved, prayed to grow up,
but the father-bridegroom's sword whipped down
with an unchristian sound on the river's shore of Gheel.
We say it still about too many women:
she's lost her head.
She has stayed with me for many years, now, patron of
mental illness and menopause.

In the dining room, look up!
Joseph of Cupertino floats on the ceiling
simple with love.

The saints in the house will not eat tonight, no matter
the shouts, the leaps toward dinner floating by the vigas.

Out in the garden, San Isidro coaxes the day lilies to stay
just a little longer, gives holiness
to the tomatoes and the squash.
His oxen furrow a bed, driven by angels
and after them comes
the bounty.

Isidro invited the Plant Divas to join him, and as they all rejoice,
the back garden explodes into fireworks of wildflowers
and color.
They whisper to marigolds and yarrow,
to catalpa and cottonwood.
Even the grasses have stories to tell,
and they all listen intently.

There are saints in this house who laugh with the Buddha
and old African magicians. They have all tried on
the little white shoes and the hats, rolled on every bed covered
in hand-stitched spreads from many countries.
It's a different point of view.

There are saints in this house who take up your burdens
just for a little while, lean down and kiss your cheek.
Can you feel their breath stir your hair?

Marie Laveau

First born in 1796, Marie Laveau was the most famous Voodoo Queen in New Orleans from 1830 to, some say, 1918. Fact points to there being at least two Marie Laveaus, the mother and the daughter; the second supposedly drowned in the St. John's Bayou flood in the late 1890s. But what's fact?

I been young for ninety years.
Was born full growed when my Mama got old,
born once more after the Bayou flood.
I'll be born again.

I live them lives just like they was my own.
I dream of Doctor John & Galpion.

I am the Hoodoo Woman,
the Voodooienne. I
skin black cats with my teeth,
eat the rooster's living heart.

I've sacrificed the goat without horns
to Papa La Bas.

I work my Gris-Gris
on all the mens and womens in this town
white or colored, ain't no never mind.
I call the numbers, me.
At midnight, I roll the Conjure Ball cross your lawn
you be dead 'fore noon if I wants.

When I Fix you, don't matter what you think
I be slippin' underneath, to the jungle
behind your eyes.

My eyes are half moons,
won't die till they're full.
They are the eyes of my mother's mother
below her seven-knotted tignon.

They are the eyes kissed three times
by Le Grand Zombie.

I got the Power, me.
I'm Marie Laveau
the twice dead Queen of Hell.

Hoodoo Death

I had me a six nights husband
a long time ago
but he died a hoodoo death.

Cotton Williams, he was a sweet
sho nuff, with his gold tooth smile
an' smellin' of bay rum, he could make
all the womens dream.
But he always come home to me.

Then this high yeller woman
she come breezin' into town
an on to his scent.
That poor Cotton Williams downwind a her
everywhere he go, couldn't shake her loose.

She be tryin' some
Get Together Drops in his sherry wine
An' Dixie Love Perfume. Blowed Drawin' Powder
in his face. Got herself a bit of Fast Luck Water
an' a Black Cat Bone. She be wearin' some Follow Me Oil,
make the Four Corners in the graveyard at night
but ain't nothin' git my Cotton come away from his ways.

So that gal, she Gris-Gris my man.
Fixed him with a Conjure Doll
An' spiders crawled outta his ears.

Each day she unwind that doll
a little more
an' Cotton's fever start to risin',
his joints swell up an' his bones be achin'.

The doctors, they say
he got the pneumonia or somethin'
so I bathe him gentle in peppermint water,
try to ease his pain with my croonin' in the dark.
But I seed them toads
come a hoppin' outta his mouth
an' I know he ain't got nothin'
the white folks can mend.

Five days,
An' the doll fall apart.

Cotton jus' lay there. Starin' at the Devil.

Them doctors, they still insistin' he died
from natural causes
but I bees seein' the ways of death honey
an' I knows this thing for sure:

Cotton Williams was a hoodooed man.

The Sineater

There were still sineaters in the South when I was growing up, and there may be yet. There was a more widespread version of this tradition back when the laying out was done at home. Hobos would not stop and beg at a house displaying a funeral wreath; they were afraid that if someone in the house passed their plate over the coffin before returning it to them, they would be forced to eat the sins of the dead.

I
The windows' shadows are staked
to the snow, hymns
chink the cracks against escape.

Miz Bessie lies inside,
weighted with bread and beer
she waits for her ticket
on the Glory Train,
waits for the Man of the Hills
to set her free.

Even time holds its breath
when the Sineater circles moonlight
and dogs go mute
before his gibbous walk.
Candles flare and dance,
night's last sound is beheaded
by the umbral image from the doorway.

The Sineater stands
waiting for his coin.

Like a *maître d'* in a fine hotel
grandpa leads him in,
a table for one
Miz Bessie's breast
laid with its stingy repast.

    II
My name is Levee Buckingham.
I am the Sineater.

My name is Levee Buckingham.
Sometimes I forget.
When the last of the old folks go
there won't be no one to remind me.
I am the Sineater.
I'd rather eat the sins of women.
They're bitter, but more like my own.
It's the strikin' back at bein' wore down
I understand.

It's easier to love them than the men.
I am the Sineater.
I have to love the dead.
Sometimes I think it was easier
for Jesus on the cross.

I was tall once, and straight,
but all those sins done bent me down.

My name is Levee Buckingham.
I used to belong to folks.
I had a Mamma and some brothers
a long time ago. But my Pa
turned Sineater
and they all went away. I live in the woods
alone.
I started with my Pa.
I was young and liked to die
even though he was the lightest one
I've had.

My Pa, he come to be Sineater
'cause he believed he had the Call
but Ma couldn't take the looks
and the skirts pulled outta her way,
so maybe she went to New Orleans
which she always wanted to see.

I used to think her sins too much
for one man to eat
but I been Sineater so long now
I wonder at her taste

I think she taste something
like this here one
full of sadness and hard times,
sins only of thought,
gettin' at the ones
who killed her dreams

I think she taste
like the sky
cryin' soft at dusk.

My name is Levee Buckingham.
I am the Sineater.
Got no one to love me
but the dead.

The Blue Folks of Kentucky

The Blue Folks of Kentucky.
Each one a memory of water,
a suggestion of salt in the air.
Some are the color of robins' eggs
and bluebell fields, a promise
of spring in the coldest winter.

Children fade into the sky,
clouds for smiles.
Nine damson plums play
in the school yard.

Bright as berries,
pale as far mountains
one step away from the gray horizon,
the blue folks of Kentucky
echo the colors of dusk
bloom on the paths,
strolling hydrangeas in any season.

Some are the exact shade
Van Gogh searched for,
cutting off his ear to see
if it was hidden there.

They are the wrong color.
Moon children, night speakers.
The envy of Druids.
Always, there is that hint
of blue. And lawless blood
choosing its own secrets
over oxygen. Genes leap

electric blue
through generations, place them
beyond what the rest of us know
or remember: the speech of gems,
whisper of ores.
Rocks lean toward them in the road,
dance grief to the soles of blue feet.

The blue folks of Kentucky
live outside our lives,
are bred for fantasy
as surely as art.

A wave hello, the luncheon special
served up and gas pumped in,
even ordinary motions are mysterious
when gestured in blue.

DNA

I am the daughter
of the Alligator Man.

When the moon is full
my teeth sing to me
in gypsy language,
words I do not understand.

Three times in my adult years
I have had them pulled
but they always grow back
louder, more insistent than ever.

We are your eye teeth,
your eye teeth,
they whisper, as the moon
marks her stages.

Our roots are deep,
deeper than yesterday
or the seventeenth century.
Egypt is nothing to us.

I lie in your arms and dream of water.

Swim though a resistance
not at all like yours, more
like the broken beads of history
enclosed in my womb,
those shards that wait to bite
your gift and hand it back.

I have been called forward
without an explanation or signifying mark
There is no obvious taint to me.

I come from the cave of the winds,
as I reach toward you
darkness drinks the gesture.

Growing again,
my teeth sing
of the river's rising.

Nobody but The Devil: A Modern Folk Tale

I

Ted Curry was crazy.
Insanity crackled off the ends of his big Irish hair,
hung in his eyes
like thick blood on a slashed neck.

Ted Curry, he loved two things:
a woman with no name
and a pig named Rose.

The woman with no name was high-strung and thin-skinned.
You could watch the blood pumping
'round her long veins like TV
but you couldn't change the channels.
No one ever heard her speak.

Some people say Rose was crazy too.
Ugly as any ordinary pig, she lived in the bathtub.
Ted Curry would dine with her,
wearing only a boar's tooth necklace
he'd eat pork chops, moanin'
Oh Rose, these are so good honey,
sooo good.
Here darlin', gnaw on this one.

He and Rose would sit on the dock,
him with his boar's tooth
her with nothing
and drink beer through the sunsets.
They liked the color their beers turned
in answer to the sky.
Sometimes Rose went to the university,

but mostly she was a homebody
just sittin' in her cool enamel bathtub
dreamin' green.

    II
August third was,
among other things,
a hot, muggy Wednesday.
And it was the day Ted Curry came home
and found
of the two things he loved, only one remained.

His woman with no name had run off Rose.

Now Ted loved his woman, but he loved Rose too.
He had no choice: the woman had to go.
But all the time he knew: a circle has two arcs.

Ted Curry searched three days in the palmetto swamp
till he found Rose.

It was late, full moon Saturday
when he chopped off Rose's head and tacked it
to the tree.

Around Rose's neck he hung the Indian bell
his woman with no name gave him
one sweet night they'd loved
under a live oak tree and the same moon.

He decorated Rose's head with pink sponge rollers
his woman left behind, then cut a circle,

two arcs of loss,
around her before knifing up
the Jack of Spades, the Queen of Hearts
and a strip of Red Cross bandage tape
sticky with drugs and love's mementos.

When he stepped back
the moon was high and calling.
He built a bonfire
large as his grief and danced 'round it til dawn:
Nobody but the Devil
can know my Baby's mind
cause nobody but the Devil
is my Baby's mind

You can bring me up
you can bring me up
but don't you
bring me down
don't you
bring me down

Then he went off to Arcadia
and got Riverbottom Fever.

III
It was 1968.
Children lit up the night in Vietnam
napalm reading lamps for the generals
and Ted Curry was crazy.
Mad enough to power an electrocutioner's dream.

He fought the dirt in the backyard of the bar.
His feet churned up the ants, made them
crazy as him, searchin' for home.

Fightin' the dirt,
he was digging up history:
Seminole villages,
America's promise to Osceola,
battle gear of the conquistadores
melted in the Florida heat.

The dirt he fought was not young.
It held the bones of Pleistocene mammals,
Jurassic dinosaurs.
Before he had beaten it,
vivacious muck clung to his boots
with the promise of a prehensile future.

Long before he won, he was fightin' a mirror.

I'm fightin' the dirt.
Fightin' the dirt.
Everybody fights each other,
big & small wars, it don't matter,
we're at it always.
So I'm fightin' the dirt
cause I don't hate nobody
but I wanna belong.

You can bring me up
you can bring me up
but don't you

bring me down
don't you
bring me down

All that fall
while the rest of us ate tacos
or went dancing or sat nervously
in the doctor's office
Ted Curry chanted:
Nobody but the Devil
can know my Baby's mind
cause nobody but the Devil
is my Baby's mind.

He was gone by winter.

    IV
It was some years later
and we'd all gone straight
but there were reports in Arcadia
of mutilated chickens and strange events.

Stories of a wild man living in the swamp.

Ladies there shivered in fantasy
and the men went out
in martial bravado.
In their WWII fatigues and their orange vests
they hunted for three days
before they caught sight
of a large feral creature.

It was late, full moon Saturday
when all their guns said what they'd come to say.

The women at home got up
as if from daydreams.
Each one shaking her head slightly,
they began to iron or cook supper
or tend the children.

All the men found was a wild boar's tooth
and the wind brushin' through the Spanish moss
whisperin'

Nobody but the Devil
can know my Baby's mind
but don't you
bring me down, don't you
bring me down.

The Weapons of Women Have Many Uses

The weapons of women have many uses.
The apple corer can kill
in between baking pies
and peeling potatoes for the Sunday social.
The grandmother fork can find a heart
as easily as a strip of bacon.

Slicing vegetables,
I think of veins
riding down the knife's edge
broad as a boulevard lined with oleander,
the poison beauty of your neck.
I travel that road in an old Cadillac
greener than thoughts, heading
through the gaudiest sunset and on
into the pocket of the night
trimmed by the lace of water oaks.

Stars and state lines slip by
under the suspiration of tires
while I fry chicken
I'm going into a far country
where the outline of the world is not a razor
peeling me down beyond bone.

On and on, faster than a scream,
smoother than a sterling silver seam ripper
with my mother's name engraved
along the sharp blade,
I drive with shadows
that cannot touch, cannot hurt,
toward a dimension further away
than putting on my nightgown, turning off the lights.

Nothing of ours is made
for the single, clean act of death.
A bed can kill anyone, and make it look like suicide.

Visiting Day at the Prison Farm

The women stand at the gate
among a clutter of children,
picnics, small presents for the men
who won't remember tomorrow
that this day was any more
than a hatch mark on the wall.
Some moment will catch them,
eyes go narrow, twitch, to see a book,
snapshot,
casual intruders to a squared space.

In a sandwich of heat and concrete,
the air gets fat
on a diet of color,
feeds on the effort of love.
Smoking cigarettes into the minutes,
bright red lips draw on the filters
a map of that forgotten country
lying between strangers, more
and less
than the distance between two turnstiles.

The guards watch the last seconds, precise
in the rules,
as the men hesitate toward the fence,
close up and milling,
back turned and alone, pacing off the clock
with the gawkiness of adolescents.

The women stir as a breeze
rearrange belts, smooth out wrinkles,
prepare their eyes for the afternoon.

FARM WIFE

I've milked this damn cow
now for years before breakfast.
Skin like old shoes, my hands do not stick
to winter metal. I move the biscuits
without flinching.

Mornings,
you pass the gravy to the space above my plate,
flick your ears like a radio knob,
report hog prices
or Brahma bulls for sale,
then flick off.

I don't care what the Farm Report says.
I want to be beautiful. I want to go to town.

Not to the Sears parts dept., not to the Feed & Grain.
I hate the John Deere man. Screw Allis Chalmers.

I want a day in the beauty parlor, a night
in the Holiday Inn.

I want to eat something I can't pronounce
off fine, candlelit linen and flirt
with each fork's waiter.

Shake the corn out of your heart!
See me.
Dance me under night's old stars,
love me again in the Confederate Jasmine.
Under memory's moon
we can be young till dawn.

A Hell of a Woman

Lilith was the first woman, made at the same time, from the same stuff as Adam. So, when Adam refused her equality and forced her to lie under him, Lilith spoke the forbidden name of God and flew from Eden. In mythology she became the Succubus, is shown as a winged woman with taloned feet. The stories differ, and I have selected from among them. Sanvi, Sansanvi, Semangelaf are the angels sent by God to bring Lilith back to Adam.

You gotta give it to Lilith,
she was a hell of a woman.

Said she'd rather
fuck demons on the beach
than lie under the belly
of that whiner Adam

& flew from Paradise.

Told God's angels to
shove it
when they came to get her back, said

Listen to me now, while you still can.
The original sin was rape
and God has chosen Adam.

From here we begin. This wound
unhealed between man and woman
draws out the world.

I am the first woman. And the last.

My children may be sterile as raisins,
die each evening with the sun,
but I continue.

You will see me soon, looking
with the eyes of sweet-faced Eve
when Adam breaks another covenant
as easily as teeth break the fruit's skin.

I am always here.
Justice owed
and justice withheld.

I see my place in history:
the forgotten metaphor
living with beasts in the desert.

You'll try to erase the sound of my name,
call me Witch.
Queen of Ghosts. Mother
of Terror.

Then you come here, wanting assurance
that I will not harm Adam's seed,
will not steal from another woman's cradle.

Go ahead. Write your names over doorways
if you think it will keep them safe.

Sanvi. Sansanvi. Semangelaf.

The syllables curl and fade,
grow old as children.

And what do you ask of me
after the eight days have set?

I am the Night Hag.

Patient as memory, I wait at the crossroads,
visit your men in that dark
they have reason to fear.
I bring them a sleep restful as my own.

Go back now. I'm through talking.
Tell God for me
this fight goes on as long as it must.
Let him make Eve, thinking to undo
this treachery. Let him make laws
declaring the mud's mistake.

In every generation
there is a woman
who belongs to me.

There's Some Eve in Every Woman
When She Eats an Apple During Boring Sex

Do you suppose she ever got it?
Ever snapped to the fact she made a bad choice?

Oh, not eating the apple. It was too delicious.
Or flirting with that snake. One bite & she knew he knew
some pretty thrilling tricks.
The tongue alone, she dreamed about for years.

No. It's Adam.

It's having to live with a man who blames you for everything:
the seasons, neckties, gefilte fish.

Do you think she heard when he swore he was innocent,
a dupe, told god how it was all her fault?
Next time, god, he says, gimme a dog.
I've had it with these chicks. They're too damn much.

Maybe she didn't hear.
Maybe she was still dreaming snaky dreams,
sniffing the directions for salt air.
Where is the beach from here? she wonders. I shudda gone off
after Lilith.

The worst of it was not leaving the garden.
No.
It was that she'd never see the snake again.
And when she looked back,
through the whirling fiery swords of the Angels,
she saw the blue of ocean, a hint of beach
behind her.

How Do Holy Women Pick Their Clothes?

I am drawn to nuns, to women
who could be nuns.
To women who have soft skin
and undershirts.
I am in love with women who wear habits or
heavy stockings and flowered dresses.
Cotton and fine wool,
steadfast in the face of modernity.

I love what holy women choose
to wear each morning. I want to know
how they decide, how they spy the dress,
the sweater. And the necklace, a gift?
Perhaps Christmas or Birthday,
perhaps just left in the room
a small box with a note that says
thank you or *I thought you would like*,
that says *love*.

How do holy women see the shoes they choose?
And the underwear?
We assume utilitarian, plain white,
the thinnest lace,
but maybe not. Maybe that's not right.
Maybe each one, underneath, has
wildly printed, beribboned and lacy
racy things that cannot be called
by that starkest of names: under wear,
but panties, bikini,
uplift and shear.

I am in love with these women
but wonder: do they like
to window shop?
Do they only go out when they need something,
is it a chore to be done?
Are they too full to look?

The Queen of Heaven Deposed

Oh, Holy Mother,
stuffed into cramped niches
behind the stubby candles of the impotent
do you remember when your womb was alive
and flamed the universe?
Do you recall the blood scent of birth
through the heavy incense of prayer?

You're dainty as a doll now,
tidy as a maid. Lacquered cheeks blush
with the lustre of dumb pearls
beneath alençon lace and blue satin
your resplendent light has dimmed
to a halo of twelve silver stars.

You've grown thin as a postcard.
Your breasts have no memory.
These thighs forget the lion's heartbeat
clasped between them, riding to war.

And who has stolen your rosary
of fifty-two skulls,
your girdle of human hands?

When beggars come
imploring intercession,
do you chafe for the Terror
that had been yours to command?
Do you wish for the storm wings
gone from your arms?

You have forgotten your own birth
and have no teeth.
Without dance, your body grew tight
and rigid, staring blind out of small spaces.
Sweet Madonna,
where is the syllable of death
in your name?

Borrowed Knowledge

The wind stirs the pages
of a lost text, and we cry   Holy Breath!

Some unknown woman appears
in dream, and we cry   Great Mother!

But,
what is it we think we know?
How deep in the body does surety go?

Do we know how to die?
Does wisdom live in our bodies
like animal fur?

Our hands fall
in an artful pose, and we cry   Sacred Mudra!

A friend appears
at the door, and we cry   ESP!

What is it
we think we know?
How deep in the body
does surety go?

How much knowledge is earned
plodding through the years,
each day tamped down
to make fertile soil?

What holds us to the earth
through hard bone,
what guides the gesture
that leaves the heart
with a dancer's grace?

What is it we think we know?
How deep
in the body
does surety
go?

New Shoes
On misreading the word "psychopomp"

   Come on Baby
git on them psychopumps! It's time to
  go dancin in the wild.

i think sequins & rhinestones
  that flamingo round your neck
  makes yr Superego look swell

Just a touch of mascara more lipstick to match
  yr nails & yr Libido's ready to prance

So grab yr kazoo sweetie let's head for the dale
   play the druidic blue Id

  While you waltz with Siggie F
  the moon & me'll rumba

  lighter than air

  ৬ ৬ ৬

  Danger!
a variation

  AUHOOGA! AUHOOGA!
    The ship's goin down!

Somebody git on them psychopumps
  try to pump out the bilge
   or we'll all be drowned
    for sure.

Basket Weaver

Proper elegance of willows
speaks of water, clear
under an old sky.
Hands bend
the shape of basket
around hours, saying this.

Ritual for the Grandmother Stick

Name the Grandmothers!
Chant the deeds
of the Grandmothers!

As you circle
in the earth circle
match your heart
to the drum
let your bracelets sound
these words
let them enter you as fire,
as water.

You have washed
in the smoke of sweet herbs
put on your skin apron
and tied the girdle, nine knots
as the Grandmothers have taught you.

Sweep the stone clean
with oak and cedar,
With raven's wing
brush the air

place salt here
and bread meal,
offer wine
to the Grandmothers
of the five directions.

Now, you begin the dance
learned in dream
the song you have brought
from the house of the Grandmothers.

It is your voice
in the song of women
that closes the circle

As you dance
Praise the Grandmothers
who have taught you this.

Take your place in the circle,
first and last

Gift of the Moon

It was the Moon
who taught us speech.
It happened in this way:

Long ago, the People
felt a sound
that could not be said
in the Owl's low hoot
or Wolf's moist howls.
It was more than the sound
the Oak makes
leaning toward water
or the click Rocks speak
in their mountain homes.

It was their own
Heart's sound they felt
and did not know how to say.
The sound of the People was missing
from the alphabet of night.

Passing over, the Moon
felt this unspoken sound
the way light feels shadow.
She felt the sorrow
of the People
who could not speak
their heart's longing
with the Loon's voice.

So the Moon came to the People.
She called the Grandmothers

and the Grandfathers
into the sacred circle.
She brought them
all the languages
the Other Ones spoke.
Their ears filled
with the speech of Crickets
and Bears, Salmon,
Plant and Tortoise.
They heard the tongues of Earth,
of Rain and Fire.

Their hearts knew a great hunger.

Each night, the circle grew
each night, the hunger grew
as the Moon brought them
the dialects of Junipers
and Jasmine, the high speech
of Eagles and Osprey.

The hunger of the Old Ones
reached out,
the hearts of the Grandmothers
and Grandfathers
tasted the night winds.

And so it was
that the Old Ones
learned Human speech:
from all the sounds
carried by the Moon

they wove our own heart's words
to fill the silence.

One there was, though,
whose heart ate only growls
and bitter sounds
so our language now
is less than praise.

Moon in the Morning

I kissed the moon this morning,
it was simply too beautiful
to resist
I could feel it on my lips
all day, until the sunset
broke open my heart.

The Girl Who Married a Dog
from an Inuit story

In this story
there is no mother.
No one to stand up
against the gifts of fur and ivory.
No one to speak what lies in the right eye,
the eye that sees what will come.

In this story
there is no father.
Only a lazy man
who would sell a girl.

A girl who refuses every boy:
this one cannot find the bear
deep in the frozen land, this one cannot sing
and where is the one who can heat me
with a single glance?

In the dark, when wishes are too easy,
this man asks for a dog as son,
a dog to turn pride into dowry.

When the dog trots in the village
that girl smells smoke, sees a wish
in those eyes.
The bridegroom has come.

Home becomes a far island
where terns ride blue air
and deer nuzzle soft lady ferns
under Nordic pines.

In their tent painted with the language of animals,
she learns to weave her husband's history in moccasin
and hide, bead, bead, quill, this is my story now.
Ancestors grow from shuttle slap,
she hears their voices on the wind, shapes them into robes
and cooking pots.

Seasons of blood pass with the moon
and the woman emerges
Widow of the Dog Husband. Mother
of rare sons.

Rising from the doorway
sunlight catches a memory walking from the sea.
She knows that shadow crawling the rocks,
hunched below screaming gulls.

Calling the name of husband,
chanting the name of each island year, she watches
as seven sons lope from deep woods.

Her heart leaps with the spring of fur and muscle.
Ancestor howls block the sun, whip the waves
and the old man falls
under another wish come true.

In this story
there is no daughter.
Only a woman returning to her village
seven sons walking tall beside her.

The Jaguar Man

"Shamans and jaguars are not merely equivalent, but each is at the same time the other." Peter Furst quoted in THE MYTHIC IMAGE by Joseph Campbell.

   I
When she went out to the porch
he was standing there, so quietly
the dog still chased rabbits in his sleep.
She shaded her eyes, wondering if he was real
or came from those night thoughts, lying
beside her husband under the framed moon,
the sweaty imprint of his desire
drying on her skin.

The man's being here
did something to the light,
bending it around the yard,
defining the emptiness
like the black outline
of a child's drawing
saved in her trunk,
like a memory worn in the arms.
And there was a smell on the air
of copal and deep jungle, the smell of sacrifice
and frangipani.

"I've come to work," he said,
"to pay off a poker debt to your husband."
The light moved with him to the woodpile,
sparkled off the axe blade like a smile.

Through the afternoon she watched
from behind the curtains

as the man moved about the place, mending
the corral, stacking hay, always with a grace
that did not speak of cities.
After supper, he disappeared with the shadows
into the mountains.

His presence wound around her all week, tighter
and tighter. She could feel her heart being squeezed
dry of sorrow, of bitterness, and where she rested
the soil turned alkali.
Soon, there would be nothing left
to hold to this place,
his last look would send her off
into the sky, windblown as spring.

And she was like a music box, waiting
for the last turn to begin the song
only he could hear.

When the night world silvered
she followed his path,
lay naked in the same meadow
and the jaguar came over her
with all the stars of night in his eyes,
his breath on her calling forth dreams
and tears she had forgotten.

   II
Fixing breakfast in a normal light,
she heard her husband come in
smelling of a week in town, smelling broke.

She stiffened as the weight of him
pressed her into the sideboard, his soiled hand
cupping the breast that did not belong to him
anymore. "Come to bed, I've been gone
all week," he said, pulling her along the hall.

She listened to the padding of the jaguar
back and forth under her window until he was done
and falling asleep.

"I have to see about the horse," she said
and escaped into day.

The man stood in the barn door
looking at her while she curried the horse
as if she were rubbing her own skin clean.
"Please," she begged,
but did not say who could help her, or how.

III

It was supper time, late and moonless,
when the dog began to bark
and whine. And there was another sound.
One that called up memories
asleep in the blood.
The woman and her husband stared,
frozen in time. Then he pushed back his chair,
"What the hell?" and the woman followed
with the shotgun into the dark yard.

The dog was curled back, hackles raised, whining
toward the barn. Jungle loam stung the air,
and somewhere parrots called in an orchid scent,
the sound of drums and sacred rattles.

As the husband started across,
the shadow bounded from a thousand year night,
uncoiled the week and leaped
for the joy of death singing to thirsty teeth.

The woman opened half the sky with double barrels,
then turned toward the mountains.

The Jaguar Man's Wife, Ten Years Later

Partway between town
and memory, I live alone.

Each day I get up
no different from other women
eat breakfast, do the chores
but as I comb my hair
no one looks from the mirror.

At night I walk in the mountains
the long-ago scent of frangipani mixes with pine.

She has married the jaguar,
they whisper in town, make the cross,
knowing not what the words mean.

I live here at the gateway to wilderness,
listen to the speech of parrots
and drums, wind and sacred smoke.
I do not easily remember
the language of town.

When the shotgun blast died away
I turned West into the mountains
sought out the Storm Mothers
as the Jaguar Man said.
I heard what the wind had to tell,
snow, flood and drought.
I've been to the other side
of rain and spoken with stars.

The Storm Mothers took me in,
taught me the languages of weather
until the padding of the jaguar
under my window.
It was time to go.

Moving North I climbed high into the blue,
seeking Eagle Mother,
goddess of dreams that come true.
She taught me flight, how to see
the smallest rabbit in the underbrush
and the vastness surrounding us.
Light and shadow each told their tale to me
while I wove the different winds into a pouch
to carry wisdom gifts from the World Mothers.
I speak air now, and know how to find home.

I dreamed and waited for the deep growl
out of the East calling me toward the sun.

Sun Mother and her Rainbow Daughters
showed me how to rise, open my arms and bow
wherever dark gives way to blazing colors.
Each dawn brought a new combination of heat
and light, a discovery turning in the braided spiral of life,
another gypsy telling the day's fortune in colors.

As I waited, I learned all the names of the Omniscient Ones,
bowed to each as I was taught. I learned the dialects of trees,
of rocks and hidden minerals.

His mating cough finally called me South, land of passion
and the full Moon. Again, we lay in mountain meadow
and spoke long the First Language of humans.
After, I told him what I had learned
since that night I learned freedom.

I have kissed the sun in every direction and the moon
in every quarter
and eighth. I know them in every season.
I ride the storm winds yet walk
through your dreams as comfort, as rest
smile when I hear you murmur, *Our Lady*.

I am joined with the Jaguar Man,
Mother to his Father in the Other World.
Here in the Between
I am not alone.
Each day I welcome
every living thing to my door yard.
I sing their Calling Songs,
weave their spirits into blankets and ponchos,
into shirts, belts and caps.

I sell these things or give them away.
Will you listen while I show you where to find
wolf or lightening in the weave?
Can you see fire's shape in this design?
Do you know by which name each is called
when you wear it thus?

No matter if you know. They surround you even so.
We are all wrapped in the love this world has for us.
Let this be your joy.

THE MIGRATION OF SAINTS

I had a dream last night,
a vision perhaps,
the great migration of saints.

All the saints rose up, stepped down
from their altars, started moving –
a great mass of love.

First came the Marys, all of Her aspects.

In the front was *La Conquistadora*,
who threw off her stiff satin and lace,
grabbed her sombrero, took up the gold braid like a lariat.
Holy *Vaquera*, she whistled up her pony
and left *La Peregrina* in charge at the cathedral.

There was the *Guadalupe*, virginal as milk,
dressed in pink with a blue cloak of stars.
Surrounded by the golden mandorla and roses,
she flew just above the ground
balancing in the hands of the angel.

Even as the seven swords of sorrow pierced
her heart, the *Mater Dolorosa* came behind.
There was nothing on the path
that did not bow down to her tears.

Our Lady of Salette, Fatima and Lourdes,
Our Lady of Perpetual Help
Annunciation Hope Snows
Mercy Victory
Consolation

Angels
Holy Souls
and Grace,
all of the Virgin Marys marched
in the vanguard

Next came the Martyrs.
Thousands upon thousands, sent out of this world
in every way there is. Too many to name but all
remembered by someone, by God.

There were the Fourteen Holy Helpers
and the Doctors of the Church.
I saw all of my favorites
so beautiful I felt my heart breaking.
I saw them all
every saint, real and imagined,
Saints from every religion
on and on and on they marched across the face
of the earth chanting *Give Peace a Chance*
in Latin and Greek, old Hungarian and French,
Yiddish, Spanish, Malay and Tagalog
all the languages of the old and new worlds
all English in my ears. Give peace a chance.

Gandhi, King, Mandela,
the flaming Buddhist monks of Tibet and Vietnam
they kept marching as old Peaceniks,
and the blackballed Hollywood writers joined up,
I swear I saw Ethel Rosenberg there, too.

In my dream, everywhere they walked
was a battleground underfoot and the spirits
rose up, reconciled at last to peace.
The bones of the innocent knit up again,
ashes coalesced for the Great Migration of Peace.

Every flower slaughtered by war,
every mouse displaced, every horse left dying
every thing destroyed stood up and said
STOP!

The Great Migration of All Saints
flowed across the globe, joined now by the living.
Give peace a chance. Are you there?

Give Peace A Chance – the great John Lennon

Small Graces

How do we pay for the small graces
we receive every day?
I'm not sure, but I start from here,
bow deeply:

Thank you for the perfect tomatoes
at the Farmers Market, made into
tomato sandwiches slathered with mayonnaise,
both sides, salt and pepper on white bread.

Thank you for the clouds that make the sunset
blaze and for pink and red dawns lighting all the directions.

Thank you for the parking meter still full enough
for my errands and for showing me
that dress that makes me look fabulous.

Thank you for the glimpses of bluest sky
behind the golden cottonwood, the one at Mabel's
that holds a bouquet of children in the crook of his arms.

Thank you for all the chartreuse in my life
and for having it be what goes with everything,
a color even my mother loved.

Thank you for the husband
who helps me in every crazy idea,
tells stories of me to everyone.

Thank you for the hum in the
deep oceans of the world that no one
knows for sure what it is, though I'm convinced
of what it isn't.

Thank you for the breeze on my face
from the dervish's skirt,
whirling past in the semá,
a different holiness arising
there in the Scottish Rite temple.

Thank you, thank you, in all the languages I do not know.

I wish I was pure enough
to say thank you on each exhale,
it's what the universe deserves for all these
small graces that surround us,
a never-ending prayer of thanksgiving.

The Maine Idyll Motor Court
for Laird

Maine moon rises
over rocks and slow water,
and this could almost be home.

There are no water oaks here
to lie under on a sweet southern night,
no Spanish moss, no camellias
or shush of tide.
The susurrus of sea oats is absent.

In the desert, the moon makes another sound,
grama grass and cooling sand.
Cottonwoods bend down over thin rivers,
salt cedars brush the air with feather duster arms.
Coyotes and cicadas define the night.

I dream of us in Maine, walking through the woods
at the Maine Idyll Motor Court.
We could have lived there for days, weeks.
The absence of stuff and history
and we're on our own.
We hike into town, buy dinner in cans,
come back holding hands.
Afterwards, we move the rocking chairs closer together,
listen to the night before we go in, turn off the light.

Jonelle Maison

About the Author

On one side, Jonelle Maison is the great-granddaughter of a fundamentalist foot-washing Baptist preacher who migrated to America as part of the Scots-Irish diaspora; on the other, she is a direct descendant of William Wordsworth.

She grew up (which took an inordinately long time) in the South, then drove herself through an ice storm to Santa Fe, NM, arriving New Year's Eve, 1973, and found herself home.

Maison loves many things, chief among them goddesses, saints and myth; she loves enlightenment, too, but so far, it's only hearsay.

Maison makes her living as a writer, a bill drafter for the New Mexico legislature, and has written, read and loved poetry for sixty years. She is the author of a romance novel and is currently working on a book collecting and re-telling the folk stories of saints, particularly in northern New Mexico.

Cruisin' Passion Boulevard

www.ingramcontent.com/pod-product-compliance
Lightning Source LLC
LaVergne TN
LVHW041258080426
835510LV00009B/783